THE PILLSBURY
DOUGHBOY'S
KIDS
COOKBOOK

Doubleday
New York • London • Toronto
Sydney • Auckland

The Pillsbury Company
Pillsbury Publications, Publisher of Pillsbury Classic® Cookbooks

Publisher: Sally Peters
Publication Manager: Diane B. Anderson
Recipe Copy Editor: Nancy A. Lilleberg
Senior Editor: Elaine Christiansen
Senior Food Editor: Jackie Sheehan
Test Kitchen Coordinator: Pat Peterson
Contributing Editor: Patricia Miller
Home Economists: Pillsbury Publications
Nutrition Information: Pillsbury Technology
Art Direction and Design: Tad Ware & Company, Inc.
Photography: Studio 3
Food Stylist: JoAnn Cherry
Assistant Food Stylist: Mary Margaret Ness
Book Editor: Karen Van Westering

The Pillsbury Doughboy's Kids Cookbook and the portrayal of the Doughboy are
trademarks of The Pillsbury Company.

PUBLISHED BY DOUBLEDAY
a division of Bantam Doubleday Dell Publishing Group, Inc.
666 Fifth Avenue, New York, New York 10103

DOUBLEDAY and the portrayal of an anchor with a dolphin
are registered trademarks of Doubleday,
a division of Bantam Doubleday Dell Publishing Group, Inc.

Library of Congress Cataloging-in-Publication Data

The Pillsbury Doughboy's kids cookbook—1st ed.
p.   cm.
Includes index.
Summary: An introductory cookbook containing recipes for snacks, beverages,
breads, sandwiches, cookies, and other dishes.
1. Cookery—Juvenile literature.   [1. Cookery.]   I. Pillsbury Company.
TX652.5.P53   1992
641.5'123—dc20   91-36092
                                                                         CIP
                                                                          AC

ISBN 0-385-23871-1
Copyright © 1992 by The Pillsbury Company,
Minneapolis, Minnesota

All Rights Reserved
Printed in the United States of America
October 1992
First Edition

A NOTE TO GROWN-UP HELPERS

Remember the first time you "helped" bake a batch of cookies or made an afterschool snack all by yourself. Introduce a pint-size chef to his or her "firsts" in the kitchen with the help of the *Doughboy's Kids Cookbook* created for kids from preschool through the early school years.

The *Doughboy's Kids Cookbook* is—**First of all, about fun!** You know the pleasure you get from making something and then serving it to an admiring family. This book will help you give that same satisfaction to children, hopefully without tears on their part or frustration on yours. Cooking is fun for just one kid or a whole bunch such as Cub Scouts, Brownies, play groups, or birthday party guests. And there is no better way to spend a rainy or snowy afternoon!

Next, about learning. With only minimum guidance on your part, making these recipes can be a learning experience in disguise for a child. Kids read the recipes, count cups of flour, and master skills like measuring ingredients, using a blender or kneading dough. Between the recipes the Doughboy offers lively food and cooking facts that can spark a child's imagination.

We have also included kid-oriented nutrition information to start the younger generation on healthy eating habits. Easy-to-understand symbols identify important nutritional aspects of foods. For your own reference, we have also included complete nutritional information in chart form for each recipe.

Then, about safety. To help youngsters work safely in the kitchen, we have included Kitchen Safety Rules. You should review this list carefully with a child before any cooking is started. There are Doughboy hats 🎩 next to some of the steps in the recipes. These are steps where you especially need to lend a hand or keep a close watch. Even so, these are recipes to grow on, and if your junior gourmet is old enough, he or she can take over some of the "Doughboy Hat" steps from you.

Finally, about success! All of these recipes are kid-tested and adult approved—not only for taste but for their how-to-ability. You can help in other ways to ensure that kids succeed. Encourage them to try new cooking skills and do as much of the recipe as they can. Don't worry that the kitchen is messy or the results aren't picture perfect. Your beginning chef won't notice. But most of all be generous with your praise so that this "first" will lead to many more kitchen successes.

We hope these ventures in "real" cooking will be as fun and adventurous for you as it is for your kitchen beginner.

The Food Editors from the Pillsbury Kitchens

CONTENTS

READY, SET, GO! 6

PLAYING IT SAFE 7

MIXING, MEASURING & OTHER NEAT THINGS 8

UTENSILS 10

FOOD = FUEL 12

CAN YOU FIND? 13

SNACKS 14–21

    Fruity Yogurt Pops   Fun Food Facts:

    Peanut Butter Bagelwiches   Where Do Raisins

    Backpack Snack   Come From?

    Ants on a Log   What Is Yogurt?

    Bugs in a Boat

BEVERAGES 22–27

    Choco-Puddin' Shake   Fun Food Facts:

    Peachy-Keen Cooler   How to "Dress Up"

    Great Tastin' Grape Juice   Ice Cubes

         How to Use a Blender

BREADS 28–35

    Sticky Pull-Apart Bread   Fun Food Facts:

    French Toast Folks   Where Does Flour

    Banana Chocolate Chip   Come From?

       Muffins   How to Knead Dough

SALADS **36–41**

Tuna Salad Cones

Chicken Salad Nests

Stegosaurus Salad

Fun Food Facts:

What Are Vitamins?

How to Shred Carrots

SANDWICHES **42–47**

Corn Dog Twists

Funny-Faced Kidswiches

Peppy Pizza Pies

Fun Food Facts:

What Makes a

Well-Balanced Meal?

How to Set the Table

PASTA & SOUP **48–53**

Creamy Mac 'n Cheese

Easy A-B-C Soup

Rings 'n Things

Fun Food Facts:

How to Cook on the

Stovetop Safely

Do You Know These

Pasta Shapes?

COOKIES **54–59**

Holiday Cookies

No-Bake Honey Crispies

Oatmeal Raisin Cookies

BARS **60–65**

Poppin' Fresh® Bars

No-Bake Granola Squares

Favorite Fudge Brownies

Fun Food Facts:

Where Does Sugar

Come From?

What Do Ingredients

Taste Like?

CRAFTS **66–71**

Craft Dough Cutouts

Pudding Finger Paints

Graham Cracker House

Fun Food Facts:

How to Roll Out Dough

How to Make Purple

and Orange

NUTRITION INFORMATION **72**

READY, SET, GO!

Oh, boy! Today is the day you get to make something in the kitchen all by yourself (with a little help from me and your Grown-up Helper)! What will it be—cookies to dunk in a glass of milk, something yummy to snack on after school or finger paints that you can really, truly eat?

This is your very own cookbook. It is filled with things you like to eat, and recipes you can make yourself—and your whole family will enjoy eating. Whatever you are going to make, there are some simple things to do before you get started.

1. Cover up. Cooking can get messy, so it is a good idea to put on an apron, or an old shirt with the sleeves rolled up. You may want to pull back your hair, too.

2. Wash your hands. Clean hands help you make clean food. Be sure to use lots of soap and water, and dry your hands on a clean towel.

3. Read the recipe. Go over the recipe with your Grown-up Helper, to be sure that you understand what you need and what needs to be done. That way you will not be disappointed when there is no sugar for your cookies after you have already started making them!

4. Gather utensils and ingredients. Place each item from the utensil list on the tray or cleared space on your table or counter. Do the same with the ingredient list. Then everything you use will be right there when you need it.

5. Clean up when you are done. Put all ingredients back where you found them, wash the dishes and put them away, wipe off counters, the table and the stovetop, and if you really want to make everyone happy, sweep the floor!

6. Be kind to the earth. Cans and foil, bottles and glass, and even plastic containers can be recycled. Sort them and put them in the proper containers. If your family doesn't recycle already, you can start a family project and get everyone involved. Then you will be doing your part to make the earth a better place to live.

PLAYING IT SAFE

The kitchen can be a dangerous place. Sharp knives, hot cookie sheets, boiling water, and all sorts of things can hurt you if you are not careful. That is why it is important to have a Grown-up Helper with you.

In the recipes you will find a hat that looks just like mine next to some of the steps. **When you see this hat** 👑 **, let your Grown-up Helper take over or watch you closely.** In addition, be sure to follow these:

Kitchen Safety Rules

1. Sharp knives. Only if your Grown-up Helper says it is okay, should you chop or slice ingredients. Be sure to use a cutting board. When you cut, turn the knife blade away from you, and keep the fingers that are holding the food away from the blade.

2. Mixers and blenders. Turn off the blender or mixer before you scrape the sides of the container or bowl, so that the scraper will not get caught in the blades. Turn off the mixer and unplug it before you take the beaters out of the mixer. Pull on the plug, not the cord when you disconnect it.

3. Pan handles. Turn the handles of any pots and pans on the stovetop toward the center of the stove so they will not tip over or catch on anything. That will help keep you from getting burned or splashed with hot food. Make sure that the handles are not over another burner!

4. Potholders. Use good, thick, strong potholders, not ones that are thin or wet, when you put something in or take it out of the oven. In fact, use a potholder when you are handling anything hot—even a baked potato!

5. Draining water. Foods like macaroni are cooked in lots of boiling water. All that water makes the saucepan heavy, and the boiling water makes steam that could burn you. Your Grown-up Helper needs to be there and lend you a hand.

6. Microwave tips and precautions. Foods that are cooked in a microwave oven can get very hot, especially if they are covered during cooking. Use potholders to remove dishes from the microwave. Lift the edge of the cover away from you first when removing a lid or cover from dishes. Be sure to use the right dishes, like microwave-safe plastic or glass. Do not use metal pans or foil.

MIXING, MEASURING AND OTHER NEAT THINGS

When you learned how to ride a bike, you had to hold the front wheel steady and pedal evenly to keep it going. Learning to cook is just like learning to ride a bike. You need to know how to do certain things right for the recipe to turn out good.

The following special cooking terms and techniques are used over and over in all types of recipes:

Beat. Make mixture smooth by mixing over and over with a spoon or fork, or around and around with an eggbeater or mixer.

Boil or simmer. When a liquid is boiling, bubbles come up to the surface and break. When a liquid is simmering, it is still hot, but there are no bubbles breaking the surface. To cook pasta, you boil the water. To cook soup, you simmer it.

Chop. Cut into little pieces with a sharp knife.

Crack open an egg. Hold the egg in one hand. Tap it firmly on the rim of a custard cup or small bowl. With your thumbs, make the crack bigger and pull the two halves of the egg apart. Let the white and yolk drop into the custard cup or bowl. Pick out any little pieces of eggshell before adding the egg to the other ingredients.

Grease. With a clean paper towel or pastry brush spread solid vegetable shortening on the bottom and sides of a pan.

Melt. On the stovetop, heat food in a saucepan over low heat just until the food turns to a liquid. If you use the microwave, be sure to use a dish (glass or plastic) that can go in the microwave. Start with a short cooking time and heat food until it just turns to a liquid. Watch what you are melting very carefully, and stir it occasionally so that it does not burn or boil over.

Mix or stir. Combine ingredients evenly using a spoon, fork or rubber scraper.

Shred. Rub foods like a carrot or cheese against a grater to make little shavings or strips. Be careful that you do not rub your fingers against the grater, too! Hold the food firmly, but keep your fingers back away from the grater. (See How to Shred Carrots on page 39.)

Measure. Different foods are measured differently.

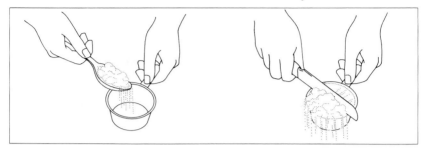

Flour, sugar, cereal. Spoon into a measuring cup for dry ingredients. Level off the top with a spatula or the straight edge of a table knife.

Baking powder, seasonings. Dip a measuring spoon into the ingredient and then level off the top with a spatula or the straight edge of a table knife.

Liquids—like water, milk, honey. Set measuring cup for liquids on a flat table or counter. Pour in the liquid. Then bend over so that you can check the amount at eye level.

Margarine, butter. The wrapper on a stick of margarine or butter has measurement markings. Cut the margarine with a table knife at the right marking.

½ stick margarine = ¼ cup or 4 tablespoons
1 stick margarine = ½ cup or 8 tablespoons
2 sticks margarine = 1 cup
4 sticks margarine = 2 cups

What equals what:

3 teaspoons = 1 tablespoon	2 cups = 1 pint
4 tablespoons = ¼ cup	4 cups = 1 quart
5 tablespoons + 1 teaspoon = ⅓ cup	2 quarts = ½ gallon
	4 quarts = 1 gallon
8 tablespoons = ½ cup	
16 tablespoons = 1 cup	

UTENSILS

WHAT DOES THIS DO?

What is a rubber scraper? Do you know what an eggbeater looks like? If not, you can check the picture list of all the utensils you will be using in the recipes. If you get to a recipe and cannot remember what a paring knife or colander is, you can look back here.

LARGE BOWL
FOR MIXER

RUBBER SCRAPER

LARGE BOWL
MEDIUM BOWL
SMALL BOWL
CUSTARD CUP

ROLLING PIN

LARGE SAUCEPAN
(OR DUTCH OVEN)
MEDIUM SAUCEPAN
SMALL SAUCEPAN

LARGE SKILLET
SMALL SKILLET

ICE CREAM
SCOOP

MEASURING
SPOONS

PASTRY
BRUSH

SCISSORS

PANCAKE
TURNER

RULER

DRY MEASURING CUPS

LIQUID
MEASURING CUP

GRIDDLE

PIE PAN

WIRE RACK

MUFFIN PAN

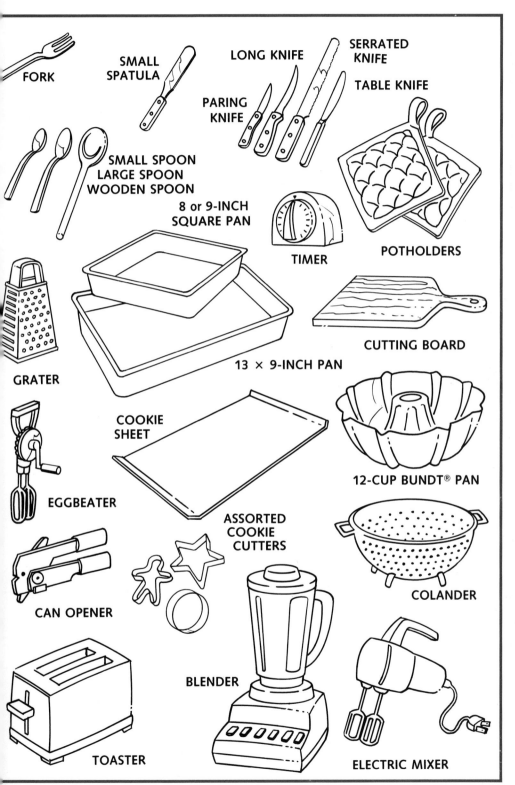

FORK

SMALL SPATULA

LONG KNIFE

SERRATED KNIFE

PARING KNIFE

TABLE KNIFE

SMALL SPOON
LARGE SPOON
WOODEN SPOON

8 or 9-INCH SQUARE PAN

TIMER

POTHOLDERS

GRATER

13 × 9-INCH PAN

CUTTING BOARD

COOKIE SHEET

12-CUP BUNDT® PAN

EGGBEATER

CAN OPENER

ASSORTED COOKIE CUTTERS

COLANDER

TOASTER

BLENDER

ELECTRIC MIXER

FOOD = FUEL

Food gives your body get up and go power. Your body is like a race car. It needs the right fuel to help you grow big and strong, jump higher and run faster. But where does your body get this "fuel," or "nutrients" as grown-ups call them, and just what do they do for you?

Protein comes from foods like chicken, hamburgers, cheese and peanut butter. It builds strong muscles so that you can kick a soccer ball harder or jump higher.

Calcium comes primarily from dairy products like milk, yogurt and cheese. You need calcium for strong teeth and strong bones so that you will grow tall and straight.

Carbohydrates come from foods like bread, potatoes and spaghetti. They give you the energy to ride your bike all day or run a race.

Vitamins are the good-food alphabet—A, B, C, D, E and K. They are found in many of the foods you eat, but some foods have more vitamins than others. Carrots have lots of vitamin A, while oranges have lots of vitamin C. Eating fresh fruits and vegetables is a great way to get the vitamins you need. With plenty of vitamins, your eyes can see better in the dark, your hair and nails will be strong and shiny, and your body will be able to do hundreds of invisible jobs to keep it running just right.

Iron is a mineral. You can find it in foods like meat and enriched cereals. Iron builds strong muscles, helps give you go-power to play all day, and makes your blood strong.

Eating a variety of foods, especially vegetables, fruit, breads and cereals, lowfat milk and other dairy products, and lean meats, is helpful in maintaining good health all your life.

CAN YOU FIND . . . ?

You have seen pictures of all the kitchen utensils you will be using, and you have seen the symbols for the different types of nutrients (fuel). Can you find them tucked into the nooks and crannies of this picture? Once you have mastered this puzzle, see if you can also find the Doughboy hidden throughout this cookbook.

Liquid measuring cup   Bowl   Carbohydrate   Knife
Dry measuring cup   Wooden spoon   Iron   Rolling pin
Measuring spoons   Saucepan   Calcium   Spatula
Cutting board   Protein   Vitamins

SNACKS

FRUITY YOGURT POPS

UTENSILS:
- 10 (3-ounce) cold drink cups
- 8 or 9-inch square pan or tray
- Can opener
- 4-cup liquid measuring cup or pitcher
- Rubber scraper
- Large spoon
- Timer
- 10 flat wooden sticks

INGREDIENTS:
1 (6-ounce) can frozen apple juice concentrate, thawed
2 (8-ounce) cartons raspberry yogurt

1. Place empty drink cups in 8 or 9-inch square pan.

2. Using can opener, open can of juice concentrate.

3. Place juice concentrate and yogurt in liquid measuring cup, using rubber scraper to get yogurt out of cartons. Stir with large spoon until well mixed.

4. Pour mixture into drink cups until each cup is a little more than half full, using rubber scraper to clean out measuring cup.

5. Place pan in freezer and set timer for 1 hour.

6. When timer rings, check to see if pops are frozen enough so the sticks will stand up. If not, set timer again for about 10 minutes.

7. When pops are partially frozen, place 1 stick in the center of each pop. Return pan to freezer and freeze pops until completely frozen, about 4 hours.

8. To serve, remove cups from pops.
10 pops

Try These Other Ideas:

Use any of the following combinations of yogurt and juice concentrate.
- Black cherry yogurt and apple juice concentrate
- Strawberry yogurt and apple juice concentrate
- Peach yogurt and orange juice concentrate
- Pineapple yogurt and orange juice concentrate
- Blueberry yogurt and grape juice concentrate
- Vanilla yogurt and grape juice concentrate

PEANUT BUTTER BAGELWICHES

UTENSILS:
- ½-cup dry measuring cup
- Measuring spoons
- Small bowl
- Rubber scraper
- Small spoon
- Cutting board
- Serrated knife
- Toaster
- Table knife or small spatula
- Serving tray or plate

INGREDIENTS:
½ cup peanut butter
2 tablespoons honey
3 bagels or English muffins
   Dried fruit bits

1. Measure and place peanut butter and honey in small bowl, using rubber scraper to get peanut butter out of cup. Stir with small spoon until well mixed.

2. On cutting board, cut each bagel in half to form 2 round halves using serrated knife.

3. Toast bagel halves on medium setting in toaster.

4. Spread peanut butter mixture on toasted bagel halves using table knife. Place on cutting board.

5. Sprinkle dried fruit bits on peanut butter mixture.

6. With serrated knife, cut each bagel half into 4 pieces.

7. Place on serving tray. Serve right away.
2 dozen (24) snacks

Try These Other Ideas:

Substitute any of the following ingredients for the dried fruit bits.
- Sliced bananas, strawberries, peaches, apples or pears
- Shredded carrots and raisins
- Drained crushed pineapple and coconut
- Chopped celery, chopped apples and raisins
- Jelly and shelled sunflower seeds
- Marmalade and cooked bacon bits
- Granola

UTENSILS:
- ½ and 1-cup dry measuring cups
- Cutting board
- Utility knife
- Large container with cover or resealable plastic bag
- Large spoon

INGREDIENTS:
½ **cup dried apricots**
3 **cups granola cereal**
½ **cup peanuts**
½ **cup candy-coated chocolate pieces**
½ **cup raisins**
½ **cup chopped dates**

1. Measure dried apricots and place on cutting board. Chop into small pieces using utility knife.

2. Place in large container with cover.

3. Measure remaining ingredients into container.

4. Stir together with large spoon.

5. Cover and store at room temperature.
5½ cups

Try These Other Ideas:

Add or substitute any of the following ingredients.
- Pecan or walnut pieces or whole almonds
- Unsalted shelled sunflower seeds
- Chocolate, butterscotch, peanut butter or vanilla chips
- Dried banana slices
- Goldfish or oyster crackers
- Chopped dried peaches, apples, figs or pineapple
- Crisp cereal squares
- Crisp shoestring potatoes
- Chow mein noodles
- Popped popcorn
- Miniature marshmallows

FUN FOOD FACTS

Where Do Raisins Come From?

What is brown and wrinkled and comes from California? Raisins, of course! But what were raisins before they were raisins?

Raisins are born as seedless grapes like the kind you eat with lunch, not the purple kind that grape jelly is made from. The grapes ripen in the sun on vines in warm, sunny states. Then they are dried in special dryers or even in the sun. As they dry, they get all wrinkly and very sweet.

What Is Yogurt?

Yogurt has been a favorite food for a long time. People all over the world eat it, especially those who live in countries such as Turkey and Greece. Yogurt is made from milk. In this country, we make it from cow's milk, but it also is made with milk from goats, sheep and horses!

The milk, along with tiny, tiny living cells, is placed in a special container and heated until the milk changes to yogurt and becomes thick.

Yogurt is yummy and can be eaten many different ways. You can eat it plain or add fruit. You can add it to a milk shake or you can freeze it like ice cream. It is good for you, too. It has the same vitamins, protein and calcium as milk.

UTENSILS:
- Cutting board
- Table knife
- ½-cup dry measuring cup
- Small spatula or table knife
- Small bowl
- Rubber scraper
- Large spoon
- Serving tray or plate

INGREDIENTS:
3   stalks celery
½   cup creamy peanut butter
1   (5-ounce) jar sharp pasteurized process cheese spread
2   tablespoons raisins

1. On cutting board, cut each stalk of celery into 4 pieces using table knife.

2. Measure peanut butter, level off with spatula and place in small bowl. Use rubber scraper to get peanut butter out of cup.

3. Add cheese spread, using table knife to get spread out of jar.

4. With large spoon, stir mixture together until well mixed.

5. Spread mixture into each celery piece using table knife.

6. Arrange 3 or 4 raisin "ants" on peanut butter mixture. Place on serving tray. Serve right away, or cover and store in refrigerator for up to 2 hours.
1 dozen (12) snacks

Try This Other Idea:

Substitute 1 (8-ounce) container of fruit-flavored soft cream cheese for the peanut butter and the cheese spread. Stir in 2 tablespoons granola or chopped peanuts. Top with raisins.

BUGS IN A BOAT

UTENSILS:
- Measuring spoons
- Custard cup
- Cutting board
- Utility knife
- Pastry brush
- Small spoon
- Table knife or small spatula
- Serving tray or plate

INGREDIENTS:
2 tablespoons orange or lemon juice
3 medium apples
1 (8-ounce) container soft cream cheese with pineapple
¼ cup golden raisins

1. Measure orange juice into custard cup. Save until Step 3.

2. On cutting board, cut each apple into 8 wedges using utility knife. Cut off and throw away the core of the apple.

3. With pastry brush, brush orange juice on cut surfaces of apple wedges to keep them from turning brown.

4. Spoon cream cheese on top cut edge of apple wedge, pushing cheese from small spoon with table knife.

5. Arrange 3 or 4 raisin "bugs" on cream cheese. Place on serving tray. Serve right away, or cover and store in refrigerator for up to 2 hours.
2 dozen (24) snacks

Try This Other Idea:
Substitute soft cream cheese with strawberries or plain soft cream cheese for the cream cheese with pineapple. Top with raisins.

BEVERAGES

GREAT TASTIN' GRAPE JUICE

UTENSILS:
- Can opener
- 1½-quart pitcher
- Liquid measuring cup
- Large spoon
- Glasses

INGREDIENTS:
1 (6-ounce) can frozen grape juice concentrate, thawed
2 cups cold water
1 (12-ounce) can (1½ cups) ginger ale, chilled
Ice cubes

1. Using can opener, open can of juice concentrate.

2. Pour juice concentrate into pitcher.

3. Measure water and pour into pitcher.

4. Open can of ginger ale and pour into pitcher. Stir gently with large spoon.

5. Place ice cubes in glasses.

6. Pour juice over ice cubes in glasses. Serve right away.
4 to 5 servings

Try These Other Ideas:

Use any of the following combinations of frozen juice concentrate and carbonated beverage.
- Orange juice concentrate and orange-flavored carbonated beverage
- Apple juice concentrate and ginger ale
- Lemonade concentrate and lemon-lime-flavored carbonated beverage
- Pink lemonade concentrate and lemon-lime-flavored carbonated beverage

PEACHY-KEEN COOLER

UTENSILS:
- Can opener
- Blender
- Rubber scraper
- Measuring spoons
- Liquid measuring cup
- Glasses

INGREDIENTS:
1 (16-ounce) can sliced peaches, undrained, chilled
1 (8-ounce) carton peach yogurt
¼ teaspoon vanilla or almond extract
1 cup milk

1. Using can opener, open can of peaches. Place peaches with liquid in blender container.

2. Add yogurt to peaches, using rubber scraper to get yogurt out of carton.

3. Measure and add vanilla and milk.

4. Place cover on blender. Blend at medium speed until the mixture is smooth and bubbly, about 1 minute.

5. Pour into glasses. Serve right away.
4 (1-cup) servings

Try These Other Ideas:

Use any of the following combinations of canned fruit and yogurt.
- Apricot halves and apricot yogurt
- Pitted dark sweet cherries and black cherry yogurt
- Blueberries and blueberry yogurt

FUN FOOD FACTS

How to "Dress Up" Ice Cubes

Ice cubes can be pretty boring. They are cold and clear and they melt. But it is easy to dress up ice cubes. They are still cold and they still melt, but they look colorful in your glass. And they taste good too.

Juice cubes. Fill an ice cube tray with your favorite juice—orange, grape, apple, pineapple. For fun, mix and match flavors, put orange juice cubes in a glass of grape juice or apple juice cubes in pineapple juice.

Fruit cubes. Using a fork or spoon, crush strawberries, blueberries or raspberries in a small bowl. Spoon the fruit into ice cube trays and freeze. Try them in a glass of juice or lemon-lime-flavored pop for a polka-dotted snack.

How to Use a Blender

You do not need to shake a cow up and down to make a milk shake. There is an easier way—use a blender! Blenders make great drinks, but they can be a little scary to use, and you should have your Grown-up Helper by your side. Follow these simple steps:

- Be sure that the blender is unplugged while you are getting ready.
- Pour liquids into the blender first. Most blender containers are like big measuring cups with measurement marks along the side.
- Be sure the cover is on tight before you plug in the blender and turn it on. While the blender is blending, do not take off the cover or else your milk shake will spray all over the kitchen and your Grown-up Helper will not be happy.
- If you need to scrape the sides of the container, turn off and unplug the blender so the rubber scraper will not get chewed up by the blades.
- When you are all done, wash the container, but let your Grown-up Helper do the blade part because it is very sharp.

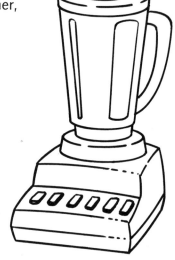

CHOCO-PUDDIN' SHAKE

UTENSILS:
- Ice cream scoop
- 1-cup dry measuring cup
- Small spatula or table knife
- Blender
- Rubber scraper
- Liquid measuring cup
- Glasses

INGREDIENTS:
1 cup softened vanilla ice cream
1 (4-serving-size) package instant milk chocolate pudding and pie filling mix
3 cups milk

1. Scoop ice cream into measuring cup and level off with spatula.

2. Place ice cream in blender container, using rubber scraper to get ice cream out of cup.

3. Add pudding mix.

4. Measure milk and pour into container.

5. Place cover on blender. Blend at medium speed until the mixture is smooth, about 1 minute.

6. Pour into glasses. Let stand 3 to 4 minutes to thicken before serving.
4 (1-cup) servings

Try These Other Ideas:

Use any of the following combinations of ice cream and instant pudding mix.
- Chocolate ice cream and banana cream pudding mix
- Vanilla ice cream and butterscotch pudding mix
- Strawberry ice cream and vanilla pudding mix

BREADS

STICKY PULL-APART BREAD

UTENSILS:
- ⅓-cup dry measuring cup
- Measuring spoons
- Small spatula or table knife
- Small bowl
- Small spoon
- Large bowl
- Wooden spoon
- Custard cup
- Liquid measuring cup
- Timer
- 12-cup Bundt® pan
- Paper towel
- Small saucepan or custard cup
- Long knife or kitchen scissors
- Plastic wrap
- Cloth towel
- Potholders
- Serving plate

INGREDIENTS:
⅓ cup sugar
⅓ cup firmly packed brown sugar
1 teaspoon cinnamon
1 package hot roll mix
⅓ cup dried currants or raisins
1 egg
1 cup water, heated to 120 to 130° F.
2 tablespoons margarine or butter, softened
Flour
Shortening
¼ cup margarine or butter

1. Measure, level off with spatula and place sugar, brown sugar and cinnamon in small bowl. Stir together with small spoon. Save until Step 14.

2. Place flour mixture from mix and yeast from foil packet in large bowl.

3. Measure and add currants. Stir with wooden spoon until well mixed.

4. Crack egg into custard cup. Add to flour mixture.

5. Measure and add *hot* water and 2 tablespoons margarine. Stir until the dough pulls away from the sides of the bowl.

6. Place dough on lightly floured surface.

7. With greased or floured hands, shape dough into a ball.

8. Set timer for 5 minutes. Knead dough by pressing, folding and turning it until timer rings and dough feels smooth.

9. Cover dough with large bowl. Set timer for 5 minutes.

10. While dough is resting, generously grease 12-cup Bundt® pan with shortening, using paper towel.

11. Measure ¼ cup margarine and melt in small saucepan over low heat or in microwave-safe custard cup in the microwave on HIGH for 30 to 60 seconds. Save until Step 14.

12. With knife, cut dough into 4 parts. Cut each part into 8 pieces.

13. Form each piece of dough into a ball.

14. Dip each ball into the melted margarine, then in the sugar-cinnamon mixture. Place balls in greased pan. Sprinkle any remaining mixture on top.

15. Cover dough with sheet of plastic wrap and cloth towel.

16. Place pan in warm place (80 to 85° F.) to let the dough rise. Set timer for 30 minutes.

17. Heat oven to 375° F.

18. When timer rings, remove towel and plastic wrap from dough.

19. Reset timer and bake bread at 375° F. for 20 to 25 minutes or until brown.

20. Using potholders, remove pan from oven and immediately turn it upside down onto serving plate. Remove pan. Serve bread warm or cool.

16 servings.

HIGH ALTITUDE—Above 3500 Feet: No change.

Bundt® is a registered trademark of Northland Aluminum Products, Inc., Minneapolis, Minnesota.

FUN FOOD FACT

What Is Yeast?

Yeast makes bread rise, or get puffy. It may not look like it, but yeast is really live, itsy-bitsy, helpful organisms (or microbes) that you cannot see. When you add water at the right temperature, they start eating sugar in the dough. That is why it is best to use yeast that is fresh and to be careful that the water you use is not too hot or too cold. While yeast organisms eat, they give off gas bubbles and these bubbles in the dough make it puff up and rise.

FUN FOOD FACTS

Where Does Flour Come From?

You use flour in all kinds of goodies—bread, muffins, cookies and cakes. But flour is really ground-up wheat. Wheat is grown on farms all over the country, especially in states like Kansas, Oklahoma, North and South Dakota, and Texas. When the wheat is ripe it turns golden brown. Then the farmer harvests it.

Kernels from the tops of the wheat are separated from the stalks. The stalks are called straw and will be used for beds for cows, sheep and horses. The wheat kernels are sent to a flour mill, where they are ground up into a fine powder—flour.

The flour is packed and shipped all over the country—and all over the world. Children in Africa and India and Russia eat bread from flour grown by American farmers.

How to Knead Dough

Kneading dough is the fun part of making bread. Kneading makes bread dough strong so that when the yeast bubbles start puffing it up, the dough will hold its shape and not fall flat like a balloon with no air.

Do you use your knees to knead? To knead dough, you use your hands not your knees:

- Clear off a flat surface like a table or counter or use a big cutting board.
- Sprinkle the surface with flour so the dough will not stick.
- Rub a light coating of solid vegetable shortening on your hands or dust them with flour so the dough will not stick to them.
- Shape the dough into a ball.
- Press on the dough with the bottom of the palms (the "heels") of your hands and push away from you.
- Fold the dough over and turn it.
- Press and push again, then fold and turn again.
- Repeat these steps for as long as the recipe says.
- After all that work, both you and the dough need a rest! You can sit down, but the dough should be covered with a large bowl while it rests.

How to Knead Dough

Shape the dough into a ball.

Press and push.

Fold and turn.

FRENCH TOAST FOLKS

UTENSILS:
- 4 or 5-inch boy or girl-shaped metal cookie cutter
- Pie pan
- Fork
- Liquid measuring cup
- Measuring spoons
- Small spatula or table knife
- Griddle or large skillet
- Pancake turner
- Serving plates

INGREDIENTS:
8 slices (½-inch-thick) white bread
2 eggs
½ cup milk
1 tablespoon sugar
¼ teaspoon cinnamon
Dash of salt
Shortening
Margarine or butter
Syrup

1. Using cookie cutter, cut out 1 shape from each bread slice. Save until Step 6.

2. Crack eggs 1 at a time into pie pan. Beat eggs with fork until foamy.

3. Measure and add milk. Measure, level off with spatula and add sugar, cinnamon and salt to eggs. Mix well with fork.

4. Heat griddle to medium-high heat (375° F.).

5. Grease griddle lightly with shortening.

6. Dip cut-out bread slices into egg mixture, turning to coat both sides.

7. Place on griddle and cook over medium heat, about 1 to 2 minutes, or until light brown.

8. Using pancake turner, turn bread over and cook other side for 1 to 2 minutes, or until light brown.

9. With pancake turner, place French toast on serving plates. Serve right away with margarine and syrup.
8 servings

Try These Other Ideas:

Use raisin, cinnamon or whole wheat bread for the white bread.

Serve with fruit-flavored yogurt or fresh fruit instead of margarine and syrup; or serve with margarine and a cinnamon-sugar mixture.

BANANA CHOCOLATE CHIP MUFFINS

UTENSILS:
- 18 paper baking cups
- Muffin pans
- Pie pan
- Fork
- Large bowl
- ½ and 1-cup dry measuring cups
- Wooden spoon
- Custard cup
- Liquid measuring cup
- Measuring spoons
- Small spatula or table knife
- Rubber scraper
- Timer
- Toothpicks
- Potholders
- Wire racks

INGREDIENTS:
3 large ripe bananas
½ cup margarine or butter, softened
½ cup firmly packed brown sugar
2 eggs
¼ cup milk
1 teaspoon vanilla
2 cups all-purpose or unbleached flour
1 teaspoon baking powder
1 teaspoon baking soda
¼ teaspoon salt
½ cup miniature chocolate chips

1. Heat oven to 375° F.

2. Place 18 paper baking cups in 18 muffin pan cups.

3. Peel bananas and place in pie pan. Mash bananas with fork. Save until Step 8.

4. Place margarine in large bowl. Measure and add brown sugar.

5. Beat with wooden spoon until well mixed.

6. Crack eggs 1 at a time into custard cup and add to brown sugar mixture.

7. Measure and add milk and vanilla.

8. Add bananas and mix well.

9. Lightly spoon flour into measuring cup and level off with spatula. Add flour to banana mixture.

10. Measure, level off with spatula and add baking powder, baking soda and salt. Stir with wooden spoon just until all dry ingredients are moistened.

11. Measure and stir in chocolate chips.

12. Spoon batter into paper-lined muffin cups, pushing batter from spoon with rubber scraper, until each cup is a little more than half full.

13. Set timer and bake muffins at 375° F. for 20 to 25 minutes or until a toothpick inserted in the center of a muffin comes out clean.

14. Using potholders, remove pans from oven. Place pans on wire racks and let muffins cool in pans for 3 minutes.

15. Remove muffins from pans and serve warm.
1½ dozen (18) muffins

HIGH ALTITUDE—Above 3500 Feet: Decrease baking soda to ½ teaspoon. Bake at 400° F. for 20 to 25 minutes.

SALADS

TUNA SALAD CONES

UTENSILS:
- Liquid measuring cup
- Medium saucepan
- ⅓ and ½-cup dry measuring cups
- Timer
- Wooden spoon
- Colander
- Can opener
- Medium bowl
- Fork
- Rubber scraper
- Large spoon
- Plastic wrap or foil

INGREDIENTS:
4   cups water
½   cup (2½ ounces) uncooked macaroni rings
1   (6⅛-ounce) can water-packed tuna
½   cup cooked peas
½   cup (2 ounces) shredded Cheddar cheese
½   cup mayonnaise or salad dressing
    Dash of salt
    Dash of pepper
6   flat-bottomed ice cream cones

1. Measure water and pour into medium saucepan.

2. Bring water to a boil over medium-high heat.

3. Measure and add macaroni to boiling water. When water begins to boil again, set timer for 6 to 8 minutes or cook macaroni to desired doneness.

4. Stir macaroni occasionally with wooden spoon.

5. Set colander in sink. Pour macaroni into colander to drain off water. Rinse macaroni with cold water. Drain. Save until Step 8.

6. Using can opener, open can of tuna and drain off liquid.

7. Place tuna in medium bowl. Break up tuna into small pieces using fork.

8. Measure and add peas, cheese, mayonnaise, salt and pepper, using rubber scraper to get mayonnaise out of cup. Add cooked macaroni and stir with large spoon until well mixed.

9. Cover bowl with plastic wrap. Place bowl in refrigerator to let the flavors in the salad blend for about 1 hour or until serving time.

10. To serve, fill each ice cream cone with a generous ⅓ cup of tuna salad.
6 servings

Try This Other Idea:

Substitute small macaroni shells for the rings, and canned chicken for the tuna.

FUN FOOD FACTS

What Are Vitamins?

Vitamins are found in every food you eat from strawberries to peas to chicken to macaroni and cheese. They do hundreds and hundreds of different jobs for your body. They help make your bones strong, your eyes sharp, your skinned knee heal.

Some foods have more vitamins than others and some have more of one kind of vitamin. You will find lots of vitamin A in carrots and squash or broccoli, and just about all vegetables are chockful of the B vitamins. Oranges, lemons and grapefruit have lots of vitamin C. Milk has vitamin D added to it to make sure everyone gets enough of that vitamin. Fresh fruits and vegetables right out of the garden have the most vitamins.

The best way to get all the vitamins you need is to eat lots of different kinds of food like fish, fruit, and French toast! Or milk, melons, muffins and mushrooms! Or pancakes, pineapple, peanut butter and pears!

How to Shred Carrots

Shredding carrots is easy, but you do have to be careful that you just shred the carrot and not your fingers.

- Use a grater and set it on a piece of waxed paper to catch the carrot shreds.
- Wash and clean the carrots.
- It helps to cut longer carrots in half so they are easier to handle.
- With one hand, hold the grater steady.
- With the other hand, hold the carrot about halfway down, and rub it along one side of the grater, either back and forth or from top to bottom.

- As the carrot gets shorter, watch your fingers. When it is really short, you get to eat that piece! Then start with another carrot.

CHICKEN SALAD NESTS

UTENSILS:
- Can opener
- Medium bowl
- Fork
- ½ and 1-cup dry measuring cups
- Cutting board
- Paring knife
- Rubber scraper
- Large spoon
- Plastic wrap or foil
- Grater
- Small bowl
- 4 serving plates

INGREDIENTS:
2 (5-ounce) cans (2 cups) chunk chicken
1 cup seedless green or red grapes
½ cup mayonnaise or salad dressing
1 small carrot
1 cup crisp chow mein noodles

1. Using can opener, open cans of chicken and drain off liquid.

2. Place chicken in medium bowl. Break up chicken into small pieces using fork.

3. Measure grapes and place on cutting board.

4. Using paring knife, cut grapes in half.

5. Add grapes to chicken. Measure and add mayonnaise, using rubber scraper to get mayonnaise out of cup. Stir with large spoon until well mixed.

6. Cover bowl with plastic wrap. Place bowl in refrigerator to let the flavors in the salad blend for about 1 hour or until serving time.

7. Just before serving, shred carrot using grater.

8. Measure out ½ cup shredded carrot. Place in small bowl. Measure and add chow mein noodles. Mix well.

9. Divide the noodle mixture onto 4 serving plates.

10. Spoon about ¾ cup chicken mixture onto each "nest."
4 servings

Try This Other Idea:

Use tuna for the chicken, and crisp shoestring potatoes for the chow mein noodles.

STEGOSAURUS SALAD

INGREDIENTS:
4 lettuce leaves
4 canned pear halves, drained
28 to 32 canned pineapple
   tidbits, drained
8 canned mandarin orange
   segments, drained
4 raisins

1. Place 1 leaf of lettuce on each salad plate.

2. Using can opener, open cans of fruit and drain off liquid.

3. Place pear halves, rounded side up and narrow end facing left, on lettuce.

4. Arrange 7 or 8 pineapple tidbits along top edge of each pear half for bumps.

5. Place 2 mandarin orange segments along each bottom edge for feet.

6. Place 1 raisin on each narrow end for eye.

7. Place salads in refrigerator until serving time.
4 servings

Stegosaurus

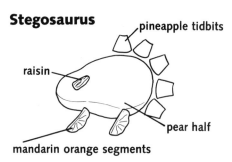

Try These Other Ideas:

Bear

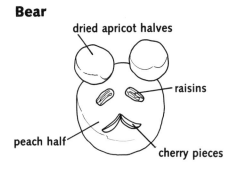

Mouse

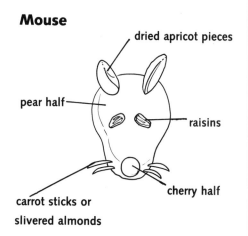

SANDWICHES

CORN DOG TWISTS

UTENSILS:
- Small sauce-pan or custard cup
- Cookie sheet
- Pastry brush
- Measuring spoons
- Small spatula or table knife
- Timer
- Potholders
- Pancake turner
- Serving tray or plate

INGREDIENTS:
1 tablespoon margarine or butter
1 (11.5-ounce) can refrigerated cornbread twists
8 hot dogs
1 tablespoon grated Parmesan cheese

1. Heat oven to 375° F.

2. Melt margarine in small sauce-pan over low heat or in micro-wave-safe custard cup in the microwave on HIGH for 15 to 20 seconds. Save until Step 6.

3. Open can of dough. Remove dough from can.

4. Unroll dough into 1 long sheet. Seal the short center perfo-ration. Separate the dough into 8 long strips (2 cornbread twists each).

5. Wrap each strip around 1 hot dog. Place on ungreased cookie sheet with the ends of the dough tucked under the hot dog.

6. With pastry brush, brush each corn dog twist with the melted margarine.

7. Measure Parmesan cheese, level off with spatula and sprinkle some cheese over each corn dog twist.

8. Set timer and bake twists at 375° F. for 12 to 16 minutes or until dough is light brown.

9. Using potholders, remove cookie sheet from oven.

10. Using pancake turner, place corn dog twists on serving tray. Serve right away.
8 corn dog twists

FUNNY-FACED KIDSWICHES

UTENSILS:
- Measuring spoons
- Table knife
- Serving tray or plate
- Cutting board

INGREDIENTS:
9 tablespoons (about 5 ounces) pasteurized process cheese spread
4 rice cakes
4 round slices luncheon meat
4 pimiento-stuffed green olives
2 small dill pickles
  Pimiento pieces from stuffed olives

1. Measure and spread 2 tablespoons of the cheese spread on each rice cake using table knife.

2. Top each rice cake with 1 slice of luncheon meat. Place on serving tray.

3. On cutting board, cut each green olive and dill pickle in half crosswise with table knife.

4. To form a face on each sandwich, use remaining cheese spread to attach 2 green olive halves for eyes and 1 dill pickle half for nose. Arrange pimiento pieces for mouth. Serve right away.
4 sandwiches

⚛FUN FOOD FACTS

What Makes a Well-balanced Meal?

Do you balance a meal by holding a sandwich in one hand and an apple in the other? Well, that is one way, but here is another.

A well-balanced meal means that you have something to eat from each of the Five Food Groups:

1. Milk, Yogurt, Cheese
2. Breads, Cereals
3. Fruits
4. Vegetables
5. Meat, Poultry, Fish, Dry Legumes and Nuts

That way you will get the calcium, carbohydrates, vitamins and protein that you need every day.

Is this a balanced lunch? A muffin, a glass of milk, macaroni and cheese, and graham crackers. No, it is not. It only has foods from the Milk and Bread groups.

How about this one? A hamburger on a bun, a glass of milk, carrot and celery sticks, and an orange. Yes, this meal has foods from all the groups.

Now it is your turn. Can you plan a balanced lunch?

How to Set the Table

Setting the table is easy, and is a good way to help grown-ups when they are busy fixing a meal. Each place needs seven things: a placemat, a napkin, a plate, a knife, a fork, a spoon and a glass. Take a look at the picture on this page. It will show you how a table setting is done.

You can make any meal extra special by picking a bouquet of flowers for the table, or you can color your own pretty placemats.

PEPPY PIZZA PIES

UTENSILS:
- 2 cookie sheets
- Paper towel
- Ruler
- Measuring spoons
- Timer
- Potholders
- Pancake turner
- Serving tray or plate

INGREDIENTS:
Shortening
1 (10-ounce) can refrigerated flaky biscuits
1 (8-ounce) can pizza sauce
1 (3½-ounce) package sliced pepperoni
1 (4-ounce) package (1 cup) shredded mozzarella cheese
2 tablespoons grated Parmesan cheese

1. Heat oven to 400° F.

2. Lightly grease cookie sheets with shortening, using paper towel.

3. Open can of dough. Remove dough from can.

4. Separate dough into 10 biscuits. Using ruler to measure, place 5 biscuits, 3 inches apart, on each cookie sheet.

5. Using fingers, press out biscuits to form 4 to 5-inch circles.

6. Form a small rim around the outside edge of each circle by pinching dough with fingers.

7. Measure and spread 1 to 2 tablespoons of the pizza sauce on each circle just to the rim.

8. Top each with pepperoni. Sprinkle each with mozzarella cheese.

9. Measure Parmesan cheese and sprinkle some cheese over each pizza.

10. Set timer and bake pizzas at 400° F. for 12 to 15 minutes or until crust is light brown and cheese is melted.

11. Using potholders, remove cookie sheets from oven.

12. Using pancake turner, place pizzas on serving tray. Serve right away.
10 mini pizzas

Try These Other Topping Ideas:
- Sliced mushrooms
- Chopped green bell pepper
- Sliced olives
- Cooked and crumbled ground beef or sausage
- Sliced hot dogs

PASTA & SOUP

CREAMY MAC 'N CHEESE

UTENSILS:
- Liquid measuring cup
- Large saucepan
- ¼, ½ and 1-cup dry measuring cups
- Timer
- Wooden spoon
- Grater
- Colander
- Large spoon
- Small spatula or table knife
- Jar with tight-fitting lid
- Medium saucepan

INGREDIENTS:
8   cups water
1¾ cups (7 ounces) uncooked elbow macaroni
8   ounces American cheese
¼   cup all-purpose or unbleached flour
2   cups milk
    Dash of pepper

1. Measure water and pour into large saucepan.

2. Bring water to a boil over medium-high heat.

3. Measure and add macaroni to boiling water. When water begins to boil again, set timer for 6 to 8 minutes or cook macaroni to desired doneness.

4. Stir macaroni occasionally with wooden spoon.

5. While macaroni is cooking, shred cheese using grater to make 2 cups. Save until Step 11.

6. Set colander in sink. Pour macaroni into colander to drain off water. Rinse macaroni with hot water. Drain. Save until Step 12.

7. Lightly spoon flour into measuring cup and level off with spatula. Place flour in jar.

8. Measure and pour 1 cup of the milk into jar. Screw on the lid so it is tight. Shake the jar until the flour and milk are well mixed.

9. Pour mixture into medium saucepan. Measure and add the remaining 1 cup milk.

10. Cook mixture over medium heat until it begins to bubble and thicken, stirring constantly with wooden spoon.

11. Stir in shredded cheese and continue cooking until cheese is melted, stirring constantly.

12. Stir in cooked macaroni and pepper.

13. Cook about 5 minutes or until thoroughly heated, stirring occasionally. Serve right away.
4 (1-cup) servings

EASY A-B-C SOUP

UTENSILS:
- Cutting board
- Utility knife
- ¼, ½ and 1-cup dry measuring cups
- Large saucepan or Dutch oven
- Measuring spoons
- Liquid measuring cup
- Wooden spoon
- Timer
- Can opener

INGREDIENTS:
1 stalk celery
½ medium onion
2 cups frozen mixed vegetables
¼ teaspoon dried thyme leaves
6 cups chicken broth
1 bay leaf
1 cup (6 ounces) uncooked alphabet macaroni
2 (5-ounce) cans (2 cups) chunk chicken
Salt and pepper

1. On cutting board, chop celery using utility knife to make ½ cup and chop onion to make ¼ cup.

2. Place in large saucepan.

3. Measure and add mixed vegetables, thyme leaves and chicken broth. Add bay leaf. Stir with wooden spoon until well mixed.

4. Bring mixture to a boil over medium-high heat.

5. Turn heat to low.

6. Measure and add macaroni. Set timer for 12 to 15 minutes and simmer soup until vegetables and macaroni are tender.

7. Stir soup occasionally with wooden spoon.

8. Remove bay leaf.

9. Using can opener, open cans of chicken. Add chicken with liquid to the soup.

10. Cook for 1 to 2 minutes, or until chicken is thoroughly heated, stirring occasionally.

11. Add salt and pepper until it tastes the way you like it. Serve right away.
10 (1¼-cup) servings)

RINGS 'N THINGS

UTENSILS:
- Liquid measuring cup
- Large saucepan
- ¼ and 1-cup dry measuring cups
- Timer
- Wooden spoon
- Grater
- Colander
- Large skillet
- Cutting board
- Utility knife
- Ruler
- Table knife
- Can opener
- Rubber scraper

INGREDIENTS:
6 cups water
1 cup (5 ounces) uncooked macaroni rings
4 ounces American cheese
2 tablespoons margarine or butter
½ medium onion
1 pound hot dogs
1 (10¾-ounce) can condensed tomato soup
½ cup water

1. Measure 6 cups water and pour into large saucepan.

🐻**2.** Bring water to a boil over medium-high heat.

🐻**3.** Measure and add macaroni to boiling water. When water begins to boil again, set timer for 6 to 8 minutes or cook macaroni to desired doneness.

🐻**4.** Stir macaroni occasionally with wooden spoon.

🐻**5.** While macaroni is cooking, shred cheese using grater to make 1 cup. Save until Step 12.

🐻**6.** Set colander in sink. Pour macaroni into colander to drain off water. Rinse macaroni with hot water. Drain. Save until Step 15.

7. Measure and place margarine in large skillet.

🐻**8.** On cutting board, chop onion using utility knife to make ¼ cup.

9. On cutting board, measure and cut hot dogs into ½-inch slices using ruler and table knife. Place onion and hot dogs in skillet.

🐻**10.** Cook over medium heat until onion is soft and tender.

🐻**11.** Turn heat to low. Using can opener, open can of soup.

12. Add soup, using rubber scraper to get soup out of can. Add shredded cheese.

13. Measure and stir in the ½ cup water.

🐻**14.** Cook until cheese is melted, stirring constantly with wooden spoon.

15. Stir in cooked macaroni.

🐻**16.** Cook about 5 minutes or until thoroughly heated, stirring occasionally. Serve right away.
6 (1-cup) servings

Try These Other Ideas:

Use small macaroni shells, elbow macaroni or bite-sized cut spaghetti for the rings.

FUN FOOD FACTS

How to Cook on the Stovetop Safely

Lots of good things to eat are made on the top of the stove, so it is important to learn how to cook on it safely. This is another time when your Grown-up Helper should be in the kitchen.

Remember:
- Do not turn any burners on until you are ready to use them.
- Choose a burner that fits the pan. Put large pans on the large burners, small pans on the small ones.
- Turn all handles toward the center of the stovetop so that the pans cannot tip over or the handles catch on anything. Be sure the handles are not over any burners, either!
- Be sure to turn the burner off before you remove the pan.
- Check to make sure that all the burners are turned all the way off when you are done.

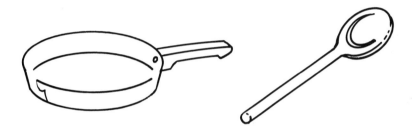

Do You Know These Pasta Shapes?

Pasta comes in a jillion shapes and sizes, like letters and shells, twists and wheels, long skinny sticks and short stubby tubes. Pasta is made out of a special kind of flour, and was invented by people in Italy and China. It can be stuffed with meat or cheese, have sauce poured over it or be used in soups and salads. You can even make things out of uncooked pasta like jewelry, nametags or pictures.

A lot of pasta names end in an "i" (that sounds like an "e") like these:
- **Spaghetti**—long skinny noodles.
- **Elbow macaroni**—short, curved, hollow noodles that look like little crescent moons.
- **Rotini**—short, twisted noodles.
- **Rigatoni**—hollow noodles about the size of your thumb.
- **Ravioli**—square noodle pockets that are stuffed with meat or cheese.

COOKIES

UTENSILS:
- Ruler
- Cutting board
- Utility knife
- Measuring spoons
- Table knife
- Cookie sheet(s)
- Timer
- Potholders
- Pancake turner
- Wire rack

INGREDIENTS:
1 (20-ounce) roll refrigerated sugar cookies
Ready-to-spread vanilla frosting, tinted your favorite colors
Candies, tinted coconut or colored sugars

1. For easier slicing and shaping of the dough, work with half a roll of well-chilled dough at a time. Refrigerate the remaining dough until needed.

2. Slice dough into ¼-inch slices on cutting board using ruler and utility knife, or measure out dough with measuring spoons.

3. Cut slices into shapes using table knife, or roll dough into balls with hands to form shapes as directed below.

4. Place shapes 2 inches apart on ungreased cookie sheet(s).

5. Heat oven to 350° F. Set timer and bake cookies at 350° F. for 7 to 12 minutes or until light brown on edges.

6. Using potholders, remove cookie sheet from oven. Let cookies cool for 1 minute on cookie sheet.

7. Using pancake turner, remove cookies from cookie sheet and place on wire rack to cool completely.

8. Decorate cookies as desired with frosting, candies, coconut and sugars.

9. Let decorated cookies set for 1 to 2 hours before storing.

Easter

Bunny: (1) Use 2 slices of dough. Place 1 slice on cookie sheet for head. (2) Cut second slice in half. Shape each half into a "petal" shape. (3) Place just touching head for ears.

Halloween

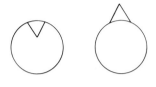

Witch: (1) Use 2 slices of dough. (2) Roll 1 slice into a ball for head and place on cookie sheet. Cut a narrow strip off each side of second slice, forming a triangle. (3) Place the 2 narrow strips about ⅛ inch from sides of head, curved edges in, to form hair. (4) Fold up curved end of triangle to form a brim on the hat. Place hat above head, edges touching.

Pumpkin: (1) Use 1 slice of dough, ½ inch thick. Place slice on cookie sheet. (2) Cut a small pie-shaped wedge out of slice. Push dough together where wedge was removed to form a round slice. (3) Place wedge, pointed end out, at top of slice to form the stem.

Christmas

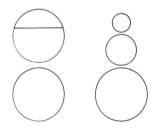

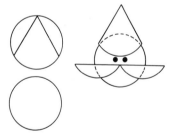

Snowman: (1) Use 2 slices of dough. Place 1 slice on cookie sheet. (2) Cut second slice in half. Roll each half into a small ball. (3) Place the 2 small balls in a row, ½ inch apart, above the whole slice to form snowman.

Santa: (1) Use 2 slices of dough. Place 1 slice on cookie sheet for face. (2) Cut a narrow strip off each side of second slice, forming a triangle. (3) Place triangle over 1 edge of face for hat. (4) Place the 2 narrow strips horizontally on either side of face for moustache, inner edges touching and curved edges down. (5) If desired, add chocolate chip eyes before baking.

NO-BAKE HONEY CRISPIES

UTENSILS:
- Waxed paper
- Cookie sheet
- ½ and 1-cup dry measuring cups
- Pie pan
- Small spatula or table knife
- Liquid measuring cup
- Medium bowl
- Rubber scraper
- Wooden spoon
- Timer

INGREDIENTS:
1 cup coconut
½ cup powdered sugar
½ cup peanut butter
½ cup honey
1½ cups crisp rice cereal
½ cup raisins

1. Place a sheet of waxed paper on cookie sheet.

2. Measure coconut and place in pie pan. Save until Step 6.

3. Measure, level with spatula and place powdered sugar, peanut butter and honey in medium bowl. Use rubber scraper to get peanut butter and honey out of cups. Stir with wooden spoon until well mixed.

4. Measure and add cereal and raisins. Stir until well mixed.

5. Using hands, shape mixture into about 1-inch balls.

6. Roll balls in coconut and place on waxed paper-lined cookie sheet.

7. Place cookie sheet in refrigerator and set timer for 1 hour.

8. When timer rings, check to see if cookies feel firm when you touch them. If not, set timer again for about 15 minutes.

9. When cookies feel firm, serve right away or place in tightly covered container and store in refrigerator.
2½ dozen (30) cookies

Try These Other Ideas:

Use chopped peanuts or about ½ cup chocolate or multicolored candy sprinkles for the coconut.

OATMEAL RAISIN COOKIES

UTENSILS:
- Cookie sheets
- Paper towel
- ¼, ½ and 1-cup dry measuring cups
- Small spatula or table knife
- Large bowl for mixer
- Electric mixer
- Rubber scraper
- Measuring spoons
- Custard cup
- Large spoon
- Wooden spoon
- 2 small spoons
- Timer
- Potholders
- Pancake turner
- Wire rack

INGREDIENTS:
Shortening
¾ **cup sugar**
¼ **cup firmly packed brown sugar**
½ **cup margarine or butter, softened**
½ **teaspoon vanilla**
1 **egg**
¾ **cup all-purpose or unbleached flour**
½ **teaspoon baking soda**
½ **teaspoon cinnamon**
¼ **teaspoon salt**
1½ **cups quick-cooking rolled oats**
½ **cup raisins**

1. Heat oven to 375° F.

2. Grease cookie sheets with shortening, using paper towel.

3. Measure, level off with spatula and place sugar in large mixer bowl. Measure and add brown sugar and margarine.

4. Beat with mixer at medium speed until light colored and well mixed, scraping bowl occasionally with rubber scraper.

5. Measure and add vanilla.

6. Crack egg into custard cup. Add egg to sugar mixture.

7. Beat well with mixer.

8. Lightly spoon flour into measuring cups and level off with spatula. Add flour to sugar mixture.

9. Measure and add baking soda, cinnamon and salt.

10. Beat well with mixer.

11. Measure and add rolled oats and raisins. Stir with wooden spoon until well mixed.

12. Drop dough by small spoonfuls 2 inches apart onto greased cookie sheets, pushing dough off 1 small spoon with the other small spoon.

13. Set timer and bake cookies at 375° F. for 7 to 10 minutes or until edges of cookies are light brown.

14. Using potholders, remove cookie sheets from oven. Let cookies cool 1 minute on the cookie sheets.

15. Using pancake turner, remove cookies from cookie sheets and place on wire rack to cool completely.
3½ dozen (42) cookies

HIGH ALTITUDE—Above 3500 Feet: Increase flour to 1 cup. Bake as directed above.

BARS

POPPIN' FRESH® BARS

UTENSILS:
- 13 × 9-inch pan
- Paper towel
- Large spoon
- ¼, ½ and 1-cup dry measuring cups
- Small spatula or table knife
- Large bowl for mixer
- Measuring spoons
- Custard cup
- Electric mixer
- Rubber scraper
- Wooden spoon
- Timer
- Potholders
- Wire rack
- Utility knife

INGREDIENTS:
Shortening
1 cup all-purpose or unbleached flour
¾ cup firmly packed brown sugar
½ cup margarine or butter, softened
½ teaspoon baking soda
1 teaspoon vanilla
1 egg
1 cup quick-cooking rolled oats
¼ cup shelled sunflower seeds or chopped nuts
1 (6-ounce) package (1 cup) semi-sweet chocolate chips or miniature chocolate chips

🌷1. Heat oven to 350° F.

2. Grease 13 × 9-inch pan with shortening, using paper towel.

3. Lightly spoon flour into measuring cup and level off with spatula. Place flour in large mixer bowl.

4. Measure and add brown sugar, margarine, baking soda and vanilla.

5. Crack egg into custard cup. Add to ingredients in large bowl.

🌷6. Beat with mixer at low speed until all ingredients are moistened, scraping bowl occasionally with rubber scraper.

🌷 7. Beat at medium speed until well mixed, about 1 to 2 minutes.

8. Measure and add rolled oats and sunflower seeds. Add chocolate chips. Stir with wooden spoon until well mixed.

9. Spread dough evenly in greased pan using rubber scraper.

🌷10. Set timer and bake at 350° F. for 15 to 20 minutes or until light brown.

🌷11. Using potholders, remove pan from oven. Place pan on wire rack to cool completely.

🌷12. Cut into bars with utility knife.
2 dozen (24) bars

HIGH ALTITUDE—Above 3500 Feet: No change.

Try These Other Ideas:

Add *one* of these ingredients to the dough in addition to the other recipe ingredients.
- ½ cup peanut butter
- ½ cup wheat germ
- ½ cup flaked coconut
- ½ cup instant nonfat dry milk

NO-BAKE GRANOLA SQUARES

UTENSILS:
- ½ and 1-cup dry measuring cups
- Small spatula or table knife
- Large resealable plastic bag
- Rolling pin
- Measuring spoons
- Large bowl
- Rubber scraper
- Wooden spoon
- 8 or 9-inch square pan
- Timer
- Utility knife

INGREDIENTS:
3 cups granola cereal
1 can ready-to-spread vanilla frosting
1 cup raisins
½ cup semi-sweet chocolate chips

1. Measure granola cereal, level off with spatula and place in large plastic bag. Seal bag tightly, removing as much air as possible.

2. Roll rolling pin over bag until cereal is coarsely crushed. Save 2 tablespoons crushed cereal until Step 6. Place remaining cereal in large bowl.

3. Add frosting, using rubber scraper to get frosting out of can.

4. Measure and add raisins and chocolate chips. Stir with wooden spoon until well mixed.

5. Place mixture in ungreased 8 or 9-inch square pan. Press in pan with back of wooden spoon.

6. Sprinkle top with the 2 tablespoons crushed cereal and press in lightly.

7. Place pan in refrigerator and set timer for 1 hour.

8. When timer rings, check to see if mixture is firm when you touch it. If not, set timer again for about 15 minutes.

9. When mixture feels firm, cut into bars with utility knife.

10. Serve right away or cover with foil and store in refrigerator.
16 bars

Try This Other Idea:

Use ready-to-spread chocolate fudge frosting for the vanilla frosting, and peanut butter chips for the chocolate chips.

FUN FOOD FACTS

Where Does Sugar Come From?

You may not believe it, but sugar comes from a beet or from a long stalk of grass.

Beets for sugar are white and they are grown by farmers in many states including Minnesota, North Dakota and Colorado. Sugar beets grow very big. They can be 2 feet long and weigh about 20 pounds!

In a factory the ripe beets are squashed and squeezed until there is no liquid left in them. This liquid turns into crystals that look like tiny diamonds when they dry, and what do you know—sugar!

Sugarcane is a long grass that grows in warm places like Hawaii. It has a thick stem and grows taller than most people. When the sugarcane is ripe, the farmer cuts it down and chops off the thick stem and cooks the stem until all the liquid comes out. The liquid dries and turns into sugar.

Powdered sugar is sugar that has been ground very fine. It is used to make frosting and can be sprinkled on brownies. Brown sugar is either light or dark brown. It still has some molasses in it, which is the liquid that sugar is made from. Brown sugar is used in cookies.

What Do Ingredients Taste Like?

When they are combined in cookies, ingredients like flour, brown sugar, baking soda, vanilla and salt taste great together. But what do they taste like by themselves?

You can conduct your own taste test of these ingredients. On a sheet of waxed paper, put a small amount of each one: flour, brown sugar, baking soda and salt. Pour a few drops of vanilla in a spoon. (You can do a taste test with many ingredients—but to be safe, don't taste raw egg.)

Now taste each one. Were there any surprises? Did the baking soda tingle your tongue?

FAVORITE FUDGE BROWNIES

UTENSILS:
- 13 × 9-inch pan
- Paper towel
- Cutting board
- Paring knife
- Small sauce-pan
- Wooden spoon
- Measuring spoons
- ¼, ⅓ and 1-cup dry measuring cups
- Small spatula or table knife
- Large bowl for mixer
- Custard cup
- Timer
- Electric mixer
- Rubber scraper
- Large spoon
- Potholders
- Wire rack
- Utility knife

INGREDIENTS:
Shortening
5 ounces (5 squares) unsweetened chocolate
¾ cup margarine or butter
1 tablespoon vanilla
2¼ cups sugar
4 eggs
1⅓ cups all-purpose or unbleached flour

1. Heat oven to 375° F.

2. Grease 13 × 9-inch pan with shortening, using paper towel.

3. On cutting board, cut chocolate into pieces using paring knife.

4. Place chocolate in small saucepan. Measure and add margarine.

5. Melt chocolate and margarine over low heat, stirring constantly with wooden spoon until smooth.

6. Remove saucepan from heat.

7. Measure and stir in vanilla. Save mixture until Step 12.

8. Measure, level off with spatula and place sugar in large mixer bowl.

9. Crack eggs 1 at a time into custard cup and add to sugar.

10. Set timer for 7 minutes.

11. Beat with mixer at medium speed until timer rings, scraping bowl occasionally with rubber scraper.

12. Lightly spoon flour into measuring cups and level off with spatula. Add flour and the chocolate mixture to egg mixture.

13. Beat with mixer just until combined.

14. Pour batter into greased pan, scraping bowl and spreading batter with rubber scraper.

15. Reset timer and bake brownies at 375° F. for 25 to 35 minutes. DO NOT OVERBAKE.

16. Using potholders, remove pan from oven. Place pan on wire rack to cool completely.

17. Cut into bars with utility knife.
2 dozen (24) bars

HIGH ALTITUDE—Above 3500 Feet: No change.

CRAFT DOUGH CUTOUTS

UTENSILS:
- Large cookie sheet
- Paper towel
- Large spoon
- 1-cup dry measuring cup
- Small spatula or table knife
- Large bowl
- Wooden spoon
- Liquid measuring cup
- Timer
- Rolling pin
- Ruler
- Assorted cookie cutters
- Potholders
- Pancake turner
- Wire racks
- Paintbrushes
- Acrylic paint and/or clear glossy polyurethane

INGREDIENTS:
Shortening
2 cups all-purpose or unbleached flour
1 cup salt
¾ cup water
Flour

1. Heat oven to 350° F.

2. Grease large cookie sheet with shortening, using paper towel.

3. Lightly spoon flour into measuring cup and level off with spatula. Place flour in large bowl.

4. Measure, level off with spatula and add salt. Stir with wooden spoon until well mixed.

5. Measure and gradually add water, stirring until a stiff dough forms. If necessary, add up to ¼ cup more water until all the dry particles are moistened.

6. Place dough on lightly floured surface.

7. Set timer for 5 minutes. With floured hands, knead dough by pressing, folding and turning it until timer rings and dough feels smooth.

8. With rolling pin, roll out dough to ¼-inch thickness, measuring dough with ruler.

9. Cut out shapes with cookie cutters. Place cutouts on greased cookie sheet.

10. Reset timer and bake dough at 350° F. for 30 to 45 minutes or until light brown on edges.

11. Using potholders, remove cookie sheet from oven.

12. Using pancake turner, place cutouts on wire racks to cool completely.

13. Spray or brush with assorted colors of acrylic paint and/or polyurethane. Let dry completely. DO NOT EAT.

TIP: The dough can be prepared ahead of time. Wrap in an airtight plastic bag and store up to 5 days in the refrigerator. For easier handling, let stand at room temperature for 10 to 15 minutes before rolling out.

FUN FOOD FACT

How to Roll Out Dough

Rolling out dough makes it flat and smooth for cookies and pies and even for making crafts. It is kind of tricky at first, but you will get the hang of it pretty quickly.

- Use any flat surface like a cutting board, table or counter. If you use a cutting board, put a damp dishcloth under it to hold the board still while you are rolling out the dough. (You can hold bowls still the same way while you are mixing.)
- Sprinkle the board lightly with flour. Rub flour on your rolling pin so that the dough will not stick to it.
- Roll the dough into a ball about the size of an orange.
- Holding the rolling pin with both hands, press down firmly on the dough and roll the pin away from you.
- Starting at the center, roll to the right, to the left and then toward you. You will start forming a flat circle. Each time you roll in a different direction, pick the rolling pin up. Otherwise the dough will roll around the pin. You may also need to flour the rolling pin again.
- Keep rolling until the dough is the thickness you need. You may want to measure it with a ruler.
- When you are cutting out shapes, use a pancake turner to lift them from the board. Add the scraps to another ball and begin rolling out a new circle.

PUDDING FINGER PAINTS

UTENSILS AND SUPPLIES:
- Liquid measuring cup
- Medium bowl
- Eggbeater or electric mixer
- Small bowls
- Small spoons
- Vinyl placemats or sheets of shiny paper

INGREDIENTS:
2 cups cold milk
1 (4-serving-size) package
   instant vanilla pudding and
   pie filling mix
   Food color

1. Measure milk and pour into medium bowl.

2. Add pudding mix.

3. Beat with eggbeater until pudding is smooth, about 1 to 2 minutes. Pudding should not be too thick.

4. If desired, place half of pudding in container with cover and store in refrigerator to use as a dessert or for painting at a later date.

5. Divide pudding into any number of small bowls. Add a few drops of food color to each bowl and stir until well mixed.

6. With fingers, paint design on vinyl placemats or sheets of paper. If painted on placemats, wash them when you are finished painting. If painted on paper, allow several days to dry.
2 cups finger paint

FUN FOOD FACT

How to Make Purple and Orange

Did you know you can make a million different colors, like magic, starting with just three—red, blue and yellow? They are called primary colors because they are the starter colors.

If all you have is red, blue and yellow food color, how do you get purple and orange?

To make purple: Use 3 drops of red and add 1 drop of blue food color. Stir together. Magic! You can make different shades of purple by changing the number of drops of red and blue.

To make orange: Use 2 drops of yellow food color and add 1 drop of red. Now you can make frosting for pumpkin cookies or cupcakes!

(Since you have gotten so good at this, I might as well tell you how to make green, too. Add 3 drops of yellow to 1 drop of blue.) Now you know the secret magic of making colors!

GRAHAM CRACKER HOUSE

UTENSILS AND SUPPLIES:
- Scissors
- Half-pint (8-ounce) milk carton, cleaned and dried (see note below)
- Tape
- 1-cup dry measuring cup
- Rubber scraper
- Table knife or small spatula
- Plate
- Cutting board
- Utility knife
- Timer
- Decorating bag and tips

INGREDIENTS:
1 cup ready-to-spread vanilla frosting
6 to 7 (2½ × 2½-inch) graham cracker squares
Assorted candies for decorating

⊕**1.** With scissors, cut off upright center seal from milk carton. Securely tape center together to form the roof.

2. Measure frosting, using rubber scraper to get frosting out of can and into cup.

3. Using table knife, spread 2 sides of the carton with a layer of frosting.

4. Press 1 graham cracker square on each frosted side of the carton.

5. Repeat Steps 3 and 4 for remaining 2 sides. Place carton on plate.

6. Fill in front and back peaks with frosting.

⊕**7.** If desired, on cutting board with utility knife, cut 1 cracker into 2 triangles to fit peaks.

8. Gently press triangles in place on carton.

9. Spread roof portions with layer of frosting. Place 1 graham cracker square on each side of roof and press in place.

10. Set timer for 10 minutes and let frosting dry.

⊕**11.** Place any remaining frosting in decorating bag with star tip or open tip.

12. When timer rings, decorate house with frosting and candies as desired, using frosting to secure candies.

1 house

NOTE: If a half-pint milk carton is not available, a 1-quart carton can be used. Cut 5 inches off the bottom of the carton, making sure edges are level.

NUTRITION INFORMATION

RECIPES	Calories	Protein (g)	Carbo. (g)	Fat (g)	Vitamin A (%)	Vitamin C (%)	Calcium (%)	Iron (%)
Ants on a Log (p. 20)	100	5	5	8	2	0	6	0
Backpack Snack (p. 18)	150	3	21	7	4	0	2	6
Banana Choc. Chip Muffins (p. 35)	170	3	25	8	4	2	2	6
Bugs in a Boat (p. 21)	45	1	5	3	2	2	0	0
Chicken Salad Nests (p. 40)	410	17	16	31	80	10	2	10
Choco-Puddin' Shake (p. 27)	260	8	42	8	10	2	35	4
Corn Dog Twists (p. 44)	300	8	18	22	0	15	2	8
Creamy Mac 'n Cheese (p. 50)	490	24	50	21	20	0	50	15
Easy A-B-C Soup (p. 51)	160	12	19	3	30	4	2	10
Favorite Fudge Brownies (p. 65)	190	2	26	10	4	0	0	4
French Toast Folks (p. 34)	210	4	24	11	6	0	4	4
Fruity Yogurt Pops (p. 16)	80	2	17	1	0	0	6	0
Funny-Faced Kidswiches (p. 45)	230	10	12	15	8	10	20	4
Great Tastin' Grape Juice (p. 24)	100	0	26	0	0	60	0	0
Holiday Cookies—Witch (p. 56)	200	1	32	8	0	0	0	2
No-Bake Granola Squares (p. 63)	280	3	43	13	0	0	2	6
No-Bake Honey Crispies (p. 58)	70	1	12	3	0	0	0	0
Oatmeal Raisin Cookies (p. 59)	70	1	10	3	0	0	0	0
Peachy-Keen Cooler (p. 25)	150	5	30	2	10	6	15	2
Peanut Butter Bagelwiches (p. 17)	60	2	8	3	0	0	0	0
Peppy Pizza Pies (p. 47)	200	8	15	12	4	2	10	6
Poppin' Fresh® Bars (p. 62)	140	2	17	8	2	0	0	4
Rings 'n Things (p. 52)	470	17	27	33	10	50	15	15
Stegosaurus Salad (p. 41)	16	0	4	0	2	8	0	0
Sticky Pull-Apart Bread (p. 30)	210	4	33	7	4	0	0	8
Tuna Salad Cones (p. 38)	300	13	21	18	4	2	10	10